A Wisley

Vegetable Varieties for the Gardener

J. W. CHOWINGS
Head of Vegetables and Ornamentals Department, NIAB

M. J. DAY
Head of Vegetable Trials Section, NIAB

Cassell

The Royal Horticultural Society

THE ROYAL HORTICULTURAL SOCIETY

Cassell Educational Limited
Villiers House, 41/47 Strand
London WC2N 5JE
for the Royal Horticultural Society

First published 1990
Second edition 1992

British Library Cataloguing in Publication Data

Chowings, J. W.
  Vegetable varieties for the gardener.
  1. Great Britain. Gardens. Vegetables. Varieties
  I. Title   II. Series
  635'.047'0941

  ISBN 0–304–32017–X

Photographs by G. Gates and A. Tiley/NIAB, Jacqui Hurst and Wilf Halliday/RHS
The contributions of Miss L. Cooper, T. Dixon, J. L. Evans,
J. Higgins, Dr R. Holland, S. Kerr, Dr J. Sweet and
Miss C. M. Thomson in the preparation of this book are acknowledged.

Every effort has been made by the NIAB to ensure the
accuracy of the information published, but no liability
can be accepted for any loss or damage suffered as a
result of its use.

Phototypesetting by Chapterhouse Ltd, Formby
Printed in Hong Kong by Wing King Tong Co. Ltd

Cover: potatoes, cabbages, parsley, onions and carrots growing together in a well-stocked
vegetable plot.
  Photograph by Photos Horticultural
p.1: the Model Vegetable Garden, Wisley, in autumn: always a source of interest.
  Photograph by Harry Smith Collection
Back cover: red cabbage 'Ruby Ball' matures in summer.
  Photograph by Jacqui Hurst/RHS

Contents

Introduction

The aim of this book is to provide gardeners with up-to-date information on vegetable varieties which are currently available in catalogues. The information is mainly derived from trials grown by the National Institute of Agricultural Botany, which has been testing vegetable and potato varieties for many years with the object of encouraging use of the best ones.

Although the work of the NIAB is primarily designed to assist commercial growers, it is also relevant and interesting to gardeners. Choosing a variety to grow in the garden is not easy and descriptions in catalogues are often incomplete. Nor is it possible to recommend the best variety of any particular vegetable, because this can vary so much with local conditions and needs. It is hoped, however, that this book will enable gardeners to compare and assess the varieties available; and that it may also suggest some new varieties to try in place of the traditional ones.

THE IMPORTANCE OF THE CHOICE OF VARIETY

Recent years have seen a great increase in vegetable growing in gardens and it is sensible for the gardener, as well as the commercial grower, to take advantage of new developments in breeding. The choice of variety is one of the major factors in achieving a good yield of produce of satisfactory quality. The use of the wrong variety for a particular season or situation could result in a poor crop or even complete failure, whereas the right variety can give very high yields and excellent quality.

Plant breeders have been making great efforts, with considerable success, to produce new and better varieties of all crops. Although most of their work is aimed at the commercial grower, the requirements of the gardener are generally similar, that is, higher yields, improved performance, greater disease-resistance and better quality.

In the United Kingdom, we can utilize varieties produced by plant breeders throughout the world. British plant breeders are providing new varieties of Brussels sprouts, cabbage, cauliflower,

Growing vegetables at closer than normal spacing is ideal for small gardens. These are in the Model Vegetable Garden at Wisley

carrots, peas and potatoes; Dutch breeders are working on the same crops, as well as onions, leeks and lettuce; and the Japanese have made some significant contributions in cabbage, calabrese and over-wintering onions. The USA is a source of new varieties of peas, dwarf French beans and sweet corn; and Australia and Denmark have provided varieties of autumn cauliflower and leeks respectively.

HOW NEW VARIETIES ARE PRODUCED

In vegetable breeding, a major development over the last 20 years has been the introduction of hybrids. A hybrid is produced by cross-pollinating inbred lines, which are derived from plants selected for particular characteristics and then self-pollinated for a number of generations. The resulting hybrid has increased vigour and uniformity, in addition to other desired characteristics, such as higher yield or disease-resistance. One apparent disadvantage, from the gardener's point of view, is that hybrid plants tend to mature at the same time. A very important point to remember is that seed should never be saved from hybrid plants because the resulting crop will be highly variable and will not be typical of the original hybrid.

The technique of hybridisation contrasts with that used for producing the traditional open-pollinated variety, which is achieved by allowing a large population with similar characters to cross-pollinate. The resulting variety consists of a population in which a large proportion of the plants have the desired characteristics but is overall less uniform than an F_1 hybrid.

In potato breeding, the traditional method is artificially to cross-pollinate the flowers of the two selected parents and to grow the seeds from the resulting berries. Each seed will produce a new variety, which may bear scant resemblance to either parent. As the potato plant is normally reproduced vegetatively via the tubers, little further variation occurs. However, there are many characters to be considered in selecting the best potato varieties and this is where the skill and practice of the potato breeder lies.

THE QUALITY OF NEW VARIETIES

A frequent complaint today is that vegetable varieties are not as good as they used to be because quality, especially flavour, has been sacrificed to the achievement of higher yields. However, a number of new varieties suggest that this is not so, for example, more winter-hardy Brussels sprouts and cabbage, bolt-resisting beetroot, stringless runner beans, better coloured carrots and sweet corn with higher sugar content and therefore improved flavour.

In the case of potatoes, there is no doubt that varieties currently available are potentially better than many older varieties. There have been increases in yield, reductions in outgrades (over- or undersized tubers), improved appearance and cooking quality and overall better disease-resistance.

VEGETABLE TRIALS AND THE GARDENER

The National Institute of Agricultural Botany arranges field trials and disease and quality tests of new varieties throughout England and Wales. The results of all these trials and tests are used to compile the NIAB Vegetable Growers Leaflets, which are consulted by commercial growers. Field trials are recorded in exactly the same way at each centre, so that results are comparable between centres; and because the trials are done at different sites and over several years, they allow a good picture of the variety to be built up.

The NIAB trials benefit the gardener in two ways. First, they provide a source of accurate and unbiased information about the varieties, which is of value to all growers. Secondly, they may indicate characters that are particularly useful to the gardener but of no consequence to the commercial grower – for example, the small fruits of the cucumber 'Petita', which might be attractive to the gardener but are certainly not to the grower.

Vegetable trials are also conducted by the Royal Horticultural Society at its garden at Wisley in Surrey and awards may be given to varieties as a result. These are First Class Certificate (FCC) for outstanding excellence; Award of Merit (AM) for great merit; and Highly Commended (HC). Although the number of trials is limited and they are carried out in only one place, they are extremely valuable to gardeners and growers alike.

Vegetable Varieties

EXPLANATION OF THE LISTS

All vegetable varieties described here are to be found in one or more of the current catalogues for gardeners. A number (or numbers) is given in brackets after the name of each variety, indicating the catalogue in which it appears, and can be identified by referring to the list of suppliers on p. 64. The potato varieties are available from shops, garden centres and mail order firms.

The varieties are listed under each vegetable in alphabetical order, unless otherwise stated. Awards given after trial at the RHS Garden, Wisley, since 1975, are noted (see p. 7). A full account of RHS trials can be found in the annual *Proceedings* of the Society, plus reports of trials of other vegetables not dealt with here.

Brief notes on cultivation are included. Sowing and planting dates generally apply to the whole country and, where there are differences, these are mentioned. For more detailed coverage of cultivation, see the RHS publication, *The Vegetable Garden Displayed*. For information about pests and diseases, see the Wisley Handbook, *Vegetable Pests, Diseases and Disorders*.

Certain varieties traditionally used by gardeners are absent from the lists because these have not been trialled by the NIAB, which is chiefly concerned with new varieties. Similarly, some notable vegetables like sprouting broccoli are omitted, since little progress has been made with developing new varieties. However, these will be included when appropriate in future editions.

BEETROOT

The main developments in beetroot have been the production of bolt-resistant varieties (i.e. which do not run to flower), the improvement of internal colour and the reduction in the number of white rings in the flesh of the root. A further development has been the introduction of monogerm "seed". Beetroot "seed" is really a dried flower head, called a cluster, normally containing two or three seeds; it is therefore possible for up to three seedlings to grow

Above: NIAB exhibits at the Royal Show
Below: part of the Portsmouth Field at Wisley, the main RHS trials area for flowers and vegetables

Beetroot can be harvested when it reaches the size required

from a single cluster. Monogerm varieties, however, produce only one seed per cluster, thus reducing the need for thinning seedlings after they have emerged.

The vegetable can either be sown early to produce small beetroots for use in salads in the early summer, or it can be sown later to grow larger roots during the late summer and autumn and for storage during the winter. The latter are sliced or diced and may be pickled.

Cultivation

Very early sowings can be made from March onwards, as soon as the soil can be cultivated. For this very early crop, it is important to choose a bolt-resistant variety to avoid the possibility of the crop running to flower before it reaches maturity. The summer and autumn crop is sown in May, using any variety listed.

Sufficient seed should be sown in shallow rows about 12 in. (30 cm) apart to allow seedlings to be thinned to 3 or 4 per foot (30 cm) of row.

Variety choice

Round red

Boltardy (2, 3, 5–12, 14–16) Bolt-resistant. Uniform globe-shaped roots with smooth skins, deep internal colour and free from white rings. HC 1978, AM 1986.

Detroit 2 – Little Ball (6–9, 14) Globe-shaped roots with deep internal colour and free from white rings. AM 1981.

Monopoly (2, 6, 7, 10, 13, 16) Monogerm variety. Uniform globe-shaped roots with deep internal colour but rather rough skins. HC 1986.

Regala (11) Bolt-resistant. Uniform globe-shaped roots with very deep internal colour and free from white rings. AM 1986.

Long red

Cheltenham Mono (8) Monogerm variety. Long conical roots, mostly below ground. Good bolting-resistance and storage. Internal colour and smoothness of skin inferior to round varieties. HC 1988.

Forono (6, 7, 9, 12) Cylindrical roots mostly above ground. Susceptible to bolting, so sow in May. Good colour, smooth skin. Stores well. HC 1988.

Others

Albina Vereduna (10) White-fleshed and globe-shaped. Susceptible to bolting, so sow in May. Smooth skin. Does not store well.

Burpees Golden (2, 5, 6, 7, 9–12, 14, 15, 17) Orange-fleshed and globe-shaped. Good bolting-resistance and stores well. HC 1978.

BROAD BEANS

The major improvement in broad beans has been the development of varieties with larger pods containing an increased number of seeds. This has happened both for the white and green Longpods (very long-podded varieties) and for the white Windsors (shorter broader varieties). Both types freeze well and it is claimed that freezing improves flavour.

Cultivation

For a very early crop, in May, sow 'Aquadulce Claudia' in late October or November. For maincrop, sow in February to March, to mature in July. Sow 2 seeds per foot (30 cm) in single rows 18 in. (45 cm) apart or equivalent spacing.

Aphids or blackfly are a common pest and early sowing often allows the crop to be harvested before a heavy infestation builds up. When plants are in full flower, removal of the growing tips, on which the aphid colonies first develop, also reduces the risk.

Variety choice (in order of maturity)

Aquadulce Claudia (2, 3, 8, 10, 12, 13, 15, 16) Winter-hardy and can be sown in late autumn. The beans are large and white. HC 1982, AM 1986.

The Sutton (3, 7, 14, 15, 17) Dwarf variety suitable for early cropping under cloches. Each pod produces 3–4 white seeds. AM 1982.

11

Broad bean 'Aquadulce Claudia', seen here growing in a pot

Bonny Lad (6) Similar performance to The Sutton.

Express (6, 8, 10, 12, 14) Early maturing, each pod producing 4 white seeds. AM 1982.

Jubilee Hysor (6, 7, 8) Windsor. Late maturing, each pod producing 6 large white seeds. HC 1982.

Hylon (2, 9, 15) Longpod. Late maturing, with on average 7 white seeds per pod. HC 1982.

Relon (6, 9) Longpod. Late maturing, with usually 7 green seeds per pod. FCC 1982.

Red Epicure (11) Early maturing, each pod producing 4 red seeds. Some of the colour is lost in cooking.

BRUSSELS SPROUTS

Hybrid Brussels sprouts have virtually replaced the older open-pollinated varieties in commercial horticulture. Their advantages are that all plants of a variety are very uniform, their maturity is predictable and the quality of sprouts excellent.

Cultivation

Seed should be sown thinly in a well prepared seed bed, to achieve one seedling every inch (2.5 cm) in rows 12 in. (30 cm) apart in the open garden, or 3 in. (7.5 cm) apart under cloches or in cold frames.

The best time of sowing, for harvesting in the autumn and winter, is from mid-March onwards.

To produce a crop for picking in succession as the sprouts mature, plants should be transplanted into their final positions in the garden from mid-May to early June, at a spacing of 24 × 24 in. (60 × 60 cm). Water immediately after transplanting if the soil is dry and also water in dry weather to maintain growth.

If a large quantity of sprouts is required for feezing, it is best to grow a crop specifically for this purpose, to mature in the autumn before they become blemished by severe weather. Varieties which mature from September until December should be used and planted rather closer at about 20 in. (50 cm) square. When one or two sprouts at the base of the stem have reached ½ in. (1 cm) in diameter, remove the growing point of the plant to encourage even development of sprouts on the stem. The process is known as stopping and results in uniform, medium-sized, solid sprouts, which can all be harvested in one picking.

Brussels sprouts 'Oliver', *left*, for early crops in September and October, and 'Rampart', *right*, a good Christmas variety

Variety choice (all hybrids, in order of maturity; see also p. 59).

Oliver (2, 10, 13, 16) Medium to short plants giving high yields of large, smooth, pale sprouts. Grow only sufficient to provide for early season requirements. HC 1984.

Peer Gynt (2, 3, 6–11, 14, 16, 17) Medium to short plants producing medium-sized, smooth, solid sprouts. Lower sprouts may open out if not picked as they mature. HC 1976, 1984.

Dolmic (10) Medium to short plants producing a high yield of medium-sized, smooth, solid sprouts that hold well. Resistant to lodging.

Roger (2, 11, 13, 16) Tall plants with very high yields of large, good-quality sprouts, which are fairly slow to deteriorate. Not for freezing because sprouts are large. AM 1984.

Widgeon (2, 7, 8, 9) Tall plants giving a high yield of medium-sized solid sprouts, dark green in colour and easy to pick. AM 1984.

Rampart (3, 6, 12, 14, 15) Tall plants producing medium-sized sprouts of good quality, which are slow to deteriorate. HC 1977.

Troika (6, 17) Medium-sized, mid- to dark green, round sprouts of excellent quality and which hold well on the plants. Not suitable for stopping.

Fortress (7, 8, 11, 15) Short plants producing round solid sprouts. Shows very good winter-hardiness. Not suitable for stopping.

CABBAGE

By choosing appropriate varieties, it is possible to have cabbage all the year round. Plant breeding has led to the development of numerous hybrids which are not only very uniform but have other attributes such as improved density and standing ability. A good example of the latter is 'Minicole', which can be left standing in the garden for two to three months after it has matured and still retain its quality. Winter white cabbages, if cut in November before they are damaged by frost, can be stored for winter use. Keep them covered with straw in a dry shed to protect from frost.

Cultivation

Sowing and transplanting dates, spacing and maturity times are indicated in the tables on pp. 58 and 60.

Early summer cabbage seed should be sown from mid-February under heated glass in seed boxes and the seedlings pricked out into pots or soil blocks as soon as they are large enough. Plants are hardened off by gradually subjecting them to lower temperatures until they are ready for transplanting. If this method is not carefully followed, there is a danger that all the plants will produce a flowering stem rather than a cabbage, particularly if transplanted before the third week in April.

Summer cabbage is best sown under cloches or in cold frames directly into a well prepared seed bed, in order to achieve rapid and even germination and good initial plant growth. Sow the seed shallowly in rows 3 in. (7.5 cm) apart, using sufficient to establish one seedling every inch (2.5 cm) of row.

Autumn, winter and spring cabbage may be sown in open seed beds in the garden and again care should be taken to achieve one seedling per inch (2.5 cm) of row in rows 12 in. (30 cm) apart.

Plants should be watered if the soil is dry at transplanting and to maintain growth in dry weather.

Variety choice (in order of maturity)

Early summer and summer cabbage (maturing in June to August)

Hispi (2, 3, 6, 7, 9–11, 14, 15, 17) Hybrid with pointed heads. Plants very uniform with dark green, smooth leaves. It is a most attractive cabbage. HC 1975; AM 1983, 1988.

Spivoy (7) Hybrid maturing very early, with pointed heads and Savoy-type puckered leaves. It has good eating quality.

Spitfire (6, 7, 12) Hybrid with pointed heads maturing later and standing longer than Hispi. It is very uniform with an attractive dark green colour.

Golden Cross (2, 3, 13) Hybrid, the earliest round, dark green cabbage. Heads with short internal stalk.

Derby Day (2, 3, 7, 8, 13, 14, 15) Medium green, round heads with little internal stalk. A ball-headed Primo type. AM 1975, 1988.

Cabbage 'Minicole', *left*, for late summer and autumn, and 'Wivoy', *right*, a very winter-hardy Savoy

Stonehead (2, 3, 6, 7, 12–14, 16) Hybrid having very uniform, small, round, solid heads which, after reaching maturity, will stand in the garden for a month without serious deterioration. AM 1982.

Castello (8, 13) Hybrid. Uniform, round, dense, green heads, with very long standing ability. HC 1988.

Minicole (2, 3, 6, 7, 9–12, 14, 15, 17) Hybrid with small oval heads which will stand for up to three months without deteriorating seriously. HC 1982.

Summer red cabbage (maturing in July and August)

Langedijk Red Early – Norma (6) Early maturing in July with long standing ability.

Ruby Ball (2, 7, 8, 11, 13) Hybrid maturing in August with uniform round heads. AM 1982, 1985.

Autumn cabbage (maturing October)

Rapier (3, 6, 10) Christmas Drumhead hybrid. Dense, round, dark green heads. Long standing ability.

Hawke (2, 6, 9, 13) Hybrid of Christmas Drumhead and white cabbage. It has an attractive dark green colour. Heads are rather oval but stand well in the garden. HC 1982.

Winter white cabbage (maturing from end of October to November, not frost-hardy)

Hidena (2, 3) Hybrid white cabbage with outer grey-green leaves. The oval to round heads may be used fresh, for immediate cooking or storage.

Polinius (8) Hybrid, oval grey-green large heads. AM 1980.

Marathon (16) Hybrid. Takes longer to mature than other winter white varieties, consequently stands cold weather in the garden better. Heads round, medium grey-green and dense.

Autumn red cabbage (maturing in October to November)

Autoro (3, 13, 17) Hybrid giving a high yield.

Hardoro (12) Hybrid, late maturing and suitable for storing.

Savoy × white cabbage (maturing in October to December)

Celtic (2, 3, 6–9, 11–15) Hybrid derived from a cross between white cabbage and Savoy. It has the solid white hearts of white cabbage but is more winter-hardy. In average winters, it will stand for up to 2 months without deteriorating.

Tundra (8, 10, 12, 13) Hybrid, similar cross to Celtic but more like a Savoy and later maturity. It can hold until February or March.

Savoy cabbage (maturing in October to January)

Ice Queen (11, 14) Hybrid maturing in October, with attractive bright green leaves. AM 1986.

Wirosa (2, 3, 13, 15) Hybrid maturing in December. An outstanding variety with good quality and standing ability. HC 1986.
Alaska (16) Hybrid, late maturing. Larger heads than Wivoy. Can stand cold weather well, and will hold in the garden until March.
Wivoy (6, 8) Hybrid, late maturing, with small heads. Can stand in the garden until March or April.

January King cabbage (maturing in October to December)

January King – Hardy Late Stock 3 (8, 13, 15) January King selection with medium-sized hearts, dark green tinged with deep purple.
Winterton (3, 9, 17) Hybrid cross between 'January King' and Winter White cabbage. Round to oval heads similar in colour and leaf type to January King but heavier. Not as winter hardy as January King.

Spring cabbage (maturing in April to May)

Durham Early (2, 3, 7–9, 11, 14, 15) Early variety of good quality and with a very good colour. Use for greens. HC 1987.
Avoncrest (2) Similar size and maturity to Durham Early, with nearly all plants producing medium-sized hearts. Suitable for use as greens or hearts. HC 1979, 1980.
Duncan (11, 13) A compact early maturing hybrid. Uniform dark coloured good quality hearts. Cabbage medium sized and solid when grown to produce hearted cabbage.
Offenham 1 – Myatt's Offenham Compacta (8, 16) Very good quality and colour. Use for greens and hearts. FCC 1980.
Dorado (2) Very good quality and colour, though slightly blue in younger stages. Can be used for greens or for late-maturing hearts, with nearly all plants producing small solid heads. Needs good growing conditions.
Spring Hero (2, 6–8, 11, 12, 14, 15, 17) Hybrid, round, spring cabbage maturing after the pointed varieties in June. Can produce large uniform heads. Susceptible to bolting if sown too soon.

CALABRESE

Calabrese, also known as American, Italian or green-sprouting broccoli, is a very fast-growing vegetable, with an excellent appearance and flavour when cooked. It also freezes very well. Plant breeding has concentrated on the production of hybrid varieties, in which every plant produces a head of really first-class quality.

Cultivation
Successional sowings can be made from late March to early July, giving crops from early summer into the autumn. To avoid transplanting, which can result in the premature development of small heads, seed should be sown direct in the garden where the

Calabrese 'Green Comet' is a useful garden variety with a good crop of secondary heads

plants will mature. However, late-maturing varieties can be raised in soil blocks or modules for transplanting into open ground, cropping in late summer and autumn.

To produce medium-sized heads, sow enough seed to establish one plant every 8 in. (20 cm) in rows 18 in. (45 cm) apart. Adequate moisture is vital and plants require at least 1in. (2.5 cm) of water (4 gallons per square yard; 21.5 litres per m²), as rainfall or irrigation each fortnight, to ensure a good-quality crop.

Variety choice (all hybrids, in order of maturity)

Mercedes (2, 8, 12, 16) Maturing about 75 days from sowing and producing large heads on short plants. Buds are medium-sized and dark. HC 1988.

Green Comet (2, 3, 7, 10) Maturing about 80 days from sowing and producing a high yield of heads with medium-sized uniform buds. After the central head has been harvested, small secondary heads are freely produced.

Citation (6) Maturing about 85 days from sowing. Heads are slender, blue-green and of good quality.

Emperor (7, 11, 12, 15) Maturing about 86 days from sowing. High yield of large heads. Good yield of secondary heads.

Green Belt (16) Maturing about 88 days from sowing. Produces large solid heads.

Caravel (10) Maturing about 90 days from sowing. Producing medium-sized solid heads above the level of the upper leaves of the plants.

Shogun (7, 14–17) Maturing about 95 days from sowing, this is one of the latest varieties, but produces large deep heads of good quality. AM 1987.

CARROTS

By using different varieties, carrots can be harvested from June until the winter months, when they can be lifted and stored in sand or peat in a garden shed to continue supplies until early April. Small Amsterdam Forcing carrots can be frozen whole and later-maturing larger varieties diced or sliced for freezing.

Plant breeders have been working on improving the colour of carrots and there are now available to commercial growers a number of hybrids and open-pollinated varieties with very bright, even, internal colour. These are also being offered to the gardener and some are included in the list below.

There are several different types of carrots classified by shape, size and maturity. Typical root shapes are shown below.

Cultivation

Very early crops, maturing in June, can be obtained by sowing Amsterdam or Nantes varieties in January or February and covering them with cloches or clear perforated polythene. The cover should be removed from mid- to late-April. These varieties are also the most suitable for harvesting as small finger carrots from July to September, by making successional sowings from February to April.

Chantenay Red Cored selections produce short conical carrots which mature during October and November from sowings in late April to early May. Berlicum, Autumn King and some Nantes varieties can be grown for harvesting from December onwards, from early to mid-May sowings. They produce long large carrots, the Berlicums and Nantes being cylindrical, the Autumn Kings conical.

Seed should be sown in shallow drills about ¾ in. (2cm) deep, in well cultivated soil. To produce small carrots of the early

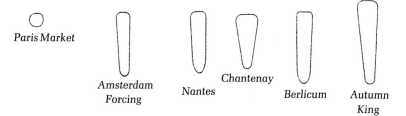

Paris Market

Amsterdam Forcing

Nantes

Chantenay

Berlicum

Autumn King

Chantenay varieties, sufficient seed should be sown to achieve about 20 plants per square foot (0.09 m²) – a population equivalent to 20 plants in 1 foot (30 cm) of row spaced 1 foot (30 cm) from the next row. Large carrots of suitable maincrop varieties can be grown by establishing 6–10 plants per square foot (0.09 m²).

Variety choice

Early (maturing in June to September)

Amsterdam Forcing – Sweetheart (11) Selection with long slender roots, good internal colour, but sometimes showing greening within the root.
Nanco (12, 17) Hybrid Nantes with uniform, smooth, cylindrical roots. HC 1980.
Nandor (14) Hybrid Nantes with uniform, short cylindrical roots. HC 1975.
Nairobi (3) Hybrid Nantes, broader and shorter with better colour than Nandor.
Nantes – Express (10, 11); **Nantes – Tiptop** (2, 6, 12, 16) Selections with medium-length cylindrical roots and good internal colour.
Parmex (6, 7, 17) Paris Market type with small globe-shaped roots. Matures very quickly. Low yielding but may be sown during spring and early summer to give successional crops.
Suko (10) A very early short cylindrical variety with small tops. It does not give a high yield, but can be used to give a series of quickly maturing crops in the garden, and could be grown in window boxes or trays. Roots cylindrical with a slight taper.

Maincrop (maturing in October to November)

Chantenay Red Cored – Supreme (10) Reliable selection with good quality.
Liberno (10) Hybrid long Chantenay with fairly broad shoulders tapering to a stumped root. Good colour.

Late maincrop (maturing from December onwards)

Autumn King – Vita Longa (3, 7, 8, 11) Conical roots with good, even, internal colour and little internal greening.
Berlicum – Berjo (8) Cylindrical roots with blunt tips and good internal colour.
Camberley (12) Berlicum type with slightly tapered roots. Deep flesh and core colour with little internal greening. AM 1986.
Cardinal (6) Hybrid Berlicum. Uniform, long, cylindrical roots.
Narman (13) Hybrid, late-maturing Nantes type with cylindrical roots and deep flesh colour.

CAULIFLOWER

In most areas, the cauliflower season can last from March or April to late November. In the southwest and southern coastal areas of Britain, winter cauliflower can be cut from December until April, although this type is susceptible to frost damage and will not grow satisfactorily in other parts of the country.

The easiest to cultivate are autumn cauliflower and winter cauliflower for spring heading, because their growing period coincides with the time when there is adequate rainfall for good plant growth. Cauliflower for maturing during the summer is more difficult to grow, requiring irrigation, as natural rainfall is usually insufficient for good growth unless the soil is of a deep moisture-retaining type.

Cultivation

Sowing and transplanting dates, spacing and maturity times are given on p. 62.

Winter cauliflower for spring heading may be sown in the open garden in a well prepared seed bed. To raise sturdy plants, sufficient seed should be sown to establish one plant every inch (2.5 cm), in rows 12 in. (30 cm) apart. After transplanting, only the minimum amount of nitrogen fertilizer should be applied in autumn to ensure development of hardy plants. In late winter, however, apply nitrogen fertilizer to promote growth.

Early summer cauliflower should be sown to establish one plant every inch (2.5 cm) in rows 3 in. (7.5 cm) apart under cloches or in frames. Seedlings should be ventilated on warm days in the autumn and late winter. The glass should be progressively removed in February and March to harden off the plants prior to transplanting.

An alternative method of raising early summer cauliflower is to sow the seed in boxes in heat in early February and prick the seedlings out into pots or soil blocks as soon as they are large enough. The plants are hardened off by gradually subjecting them to lower temperatures until ready for transplanting.

Summer, early autumn and autumn varieties should be sown under cloches or in cold frames at the same spacing as early summer cauliflower, which will ensure rapid and even plant development and reduce the risk of curd defects. Adequate ventilation must be given as soon as the weather begins to warm up, to prevent the plants growing too large and to harden them off before transplanting into the open garden. Alternatively, plants may be raised in a well sheltered seed bed in the garden.

At transplanting, plants should be watered in, if the soil is dry, and subsequently watered to maintain steady growth. At least 1 in. (2.5 cm) of rainfall or irrigation (4 gallons per square yard; 21.5 litres per m²) every fortnight is required to produce adequate growth and development of the plants.

Variety choice (in order of maturity)

Winter cauliflower for spring heading (for all areas except the southwest)

WHITE-CURDED

Asmer Snowcap March (2, 8, 12, 14, 15) Very early English Winter type which can produce a useful crop in a mild early spring. The heads tend to be shallow and loose and should be cut before they become too exposed to the risk of frost.
Walcheren Winter 3 – Armado April (3, 7, 8, 12, 14, 15); **Walcheren Winter 3 – Thanet** (9); **Walcheren Winter 4 – Markanta** (2, 3, 7, 8, 11); **Walcheren Winter 3 – Maystar** (2, 12, 13, 16) All winter-hardy in average winters. Maturing April and May and producing deep white, solid heads of excellent flavour.
Asmer Pinnacle (6,9) Late English Winter type and one of the latest, yielding consistently over the years. Heads tend to be loose and yellow.
Vilna (3, 14) Very late maturing. Heads tending to be loose, bracted and ricey.

PURPLE-CURDED

Purple Cape (2, 5–8, 10–12, 17) Maturing February and March before white varieties. Heads tend to be shallow and loose but fairly frost-hardy.

Early summer cauliflower

Montano (8, 13, 16) Hybrid, maturing about 3 months after transplanting. Very good quality but curds rather knobbly.
Alpha 3 Paloma (11) Slightly later than Montano. Vigorous plants producing well protected heads of good depth and quality.
White Summer (11) Nearly two weeks later than Montano. Very good-quality deep curds, slightly ivory in colour.

Summer and autumn cauliflower

WHITE-CURDED

Plana (8, 10, 13) Hybrid. Plants very vigorous with well protected, excellent-quality curds. All plants mature during a short period of time.
Dok (2, 3, 6–8, 10–12, 14, 15, 17) Suitable for summer crops (August) only, producing deep, well protected heads.
White Rock (2, 3, 13, 16) Slightly later maturing and requires good growing conditions, particularly adequate moisture. Produces very deep, well-protected heads. AM 1985.

Wallaby (2, 9, 12) Bred in Australia and suitable for autumn heading, maturing in the latter half of September. A Flora Blanca type, very vigorous, producing large plants with good-quality heads. HC 1985.

Barrier Reef (2, 3, 5, 8, 9, 14, 15, 17) For cutting in October. Bred in Australia, giving vigorous plants with very well protected heads which are less solid than the Flora Blanca types.

Canberra (8, 14) Very late Australian variety. Vigorous plants producing heads which are so well protected that the leaves have to be pulled back in order to find them. Heads tend to be medium-sized and loose but of a very good colour.

Serrano (16) Hybrid. For sowing in early June and transplanting in late July. Very vigorous plants with well protected heads. Maturing in late October and early November.

GREEN-CURDED

Limelight (13) An autumn variety maturing at the same time as White Rock. Smooth green curds which retain their colour after cooking.

Romanesco (2, 7, 9–12, 14) Grown as an autumn cauliflower, this variety produces green curds whose surface is a series of pinnacles. The colour and shape make it an interesting vegetable for the table.

PURPLE-CURDED

Violet Queen (9, 12, 14) Hybrid variety. High proportion of the curds useable, but rather flatter than white varieties of similar maturity. Best sown in early June and transplanted in mid July.

CELERY AND CELERIAC

Self-blanching celery can be grown without earthing up to produce well blanched, attractive sticks. Modern green varieties can also be grown in this way. Both can be used from about the end of July until frost damages the plants.

Celeriac is grown in a similar way to self-blanching celery without earthing up. It grows slowly and in October produces globe-shaped, rather rough, knobbly roots, which can be left in the ground in sheltered areas for use until the following spring, or stored in a frost-free situation.

Cultivation

The earliest celery can be grown from seed sown in seed trays under glass at a temperature of about 60°F (15°C) in mid-February. The seedlings should be pricked out into soil blocks and then gradually hardened off from April onwards. Transplant after the risk of frost has passed, from mid- to late May, spacing plants in a square at 10 × 10 in. (25 × 25 cm). This planting system ensures that the plants shade each other, aiding blanching. The crop should receive at least 1in. (2.5 cm) of rainfall or irrigation (4 gallons per square yard; 21.5 litres per m²) each week throughout its growth. Celery requires this level of moisture to maintain growth and produce succulent sticks which are not stringy.

The fungal disease *Septoria* can very seriously affect the foliage. This disease is seed-borne and is usually controlled by sowing seed which has been soaked in a fungicide.

Variety choice

Celery

Celebrity (3, 6, 8) Like Lathom Self-Blanching but slightly longer sticks.
Greensleeves (6, 10) A cross between self-blanching and green celery, producing attractive, pale green sticks. Good flavour.
Hopkins Fenlander (8) Late-maturing green celery with sticks of medium length which are very free from string. Good flavour.
Ivory Tower (7, 9) Self-blanching type with long sticks, 11–13 in. (28–33 cm). AM 1989.
Lathom Self-Blanching (11, 13, 16) Self-blanching variety resistant to bolting. To achieve string-free succulent sticks, plants must never be short of water. HC 1981.

Celeriac

Balder (3, 5, 12) Round medium-sized roots. Can be shredded or cubed and is excellent cooked or raw.

Celeriac after lifting

24

CHICORY, RADICCHIO AND ENDIVE

These are all members of the genus *Chicorium* used mainly as salad crops. They are usually associated with varying degrees of a distinctive bitter taste.

There are several different forms of chicory but the most common are Witloof, sugar loaf and radicchio. The roots of Witloof chicory are lifted in the autumn and forced in the dark to grow etiolated shoots or chicons. Sugar loaf chicory forms an elongate rather loose head resembling a cos lettuce. These are usually sweeter than other types. Radicchio or red leaved chicory has hearts with rather red leaves and white veins. These come in a range of shapes and sizes.

Endive grows rapidly with a broad, flat rosette of leaves. A useful alternative to lettuce in autumn and winter. Often blanched by covering with an upturned pot or bucket or bunching and tying up the outer leaves. There are two main types – Curled or frisées, with finely divided curly leaves, and broad leaved or Batavian with plainer wider leaves.

Cultivation

Witloof chicory is sown in May in rows 15 in. (37 cm) apart. Thin to 9 in. (22 cm). Lift roots in October and expose to the light to retard growth. Cut the foliage off above the crown and store in dry sand or soil in a cool place. To force, plant roots in sand or soil in a pot or bucket and keep in darkness at 50–60°F (10–16°C), watering as required to maintain growth.

Endive is usually sown from May to August and can be directly sown and thinned or transplanted from pots or modules at spacing about 12 to 15 in. (30–37 cm) square. Curled types can also be sown in April for summer use.

Sugar loaf chicory and radicchio are grown like endive from May to July sowings.

Variety choice

Witloof chicory

Brussels Witloof (2, 3, 5, 9, 12, 14, 16, 17) A standard forcing variety.
Normato (7, 8, 11) A Witloof variety which remains compact during forcing.

Sugar loaf chicory

Sugar Loaf (2, 9, 12, 15) Firm "cos-like" heads for autumn use.

Radicchio

Cesare (17) Small round hearts.
Palla Rossa (2, 8, 11, 15) Round hearts for autumn use.

Endive

Batavian Green (2, 9, 12) A broad, thick-leaved variety.
Green Curled (2, 3, 11) Fine, curled-leaved variety.
Moss Curled (5, 9, 12, 17) Fine, curled-leaved variety.

CHINESE CABBAGE

Chinese cabbage has been gaining popularity for use raw as a salad, or cooked, particularly stir fried in the Chinese style. Of the various kinds, the short, broad, barrel type resembling a Cos lettuce and the tall thinner Michihili type are the best known. The Pak Choi type has leaves with thick fleshy midribs.

The vegetable is very susceptible to bolting if sown before the longest day. For an early crop, therefore, choosing a bolt-resistant variety and the provision of high temperatures during the initial stages are essential. The main harvesting season is September to November.

Cultivation

Sow directly where the crop is to mature from June to mid-August, in rows 15 in. (38 cm) apart. Sow either one seed every 4 in. (10 cm) or three seeds at 12 in. (30 cm) stations, so that the seedlings can be thinned to 12 in. (30 cm) apart. Alternatively, start the seedlings in soil blocks or modules and transplant at similar distances when they have formed about six leaves.

Water the plants if the soil is dry at transplanting and to maintain growth in dry weather. Checks to growth may encourage bolting. The crop is very susceptible to pests and diseases.

Variety choice (all hybrids)

Barrel (all maturing about 55 days from transplanting)

Kasumi (6, 8) Heads tend to be loose with a short internal stalk. Very good bolting-resistance. (See opposite.)
Tip Top (2, 5, 12, 15, 17) Heavy heads with moderate bolting-resistance.
Mariko (10) Heads with good density and bolting-resistance.

Fluffy top

Eskimo (6) Attractive early maturing variety with outer green leaves and pale inner leaves protruding from the centre of the heart.

Chinese cabbage 'Kasumi' is a short barrel type

Michihili

Jade Pagoda (7) Large, medium green, rather loose heads. Long internal stalk but better bolting-resistance than other Michihili varieties.

Pak choi

Joi Choi (8, 11, 12, 16) Large heads with dark green outer leaves and contrasting white midribs. Moderately good bolting-resistance.
Mei Quing Choi (10) Green-stemmed, with moderate bolting-resistance.

CUCUMBER

There is an important difference between outdoor or ridge and glasshouse or frame cucumbers. Outdoor varieties bear fruit following pollination of the female flowers, whereas modern glasshouse varieties produce fruit without pollination. If it does take place, the fruits become deformed and the flavour is bitter. "All-female" hybrids rarely produce any male flowers. It is important to ensure that pollen-producing outdoor types are not grown close to a glasshouse in which "all-female" varieties are grown. All the glasshouse varieties listed below are of this type.

Cultivation
Sow glasshouse cucumbers singly in pots from February to May

27

and grow at a minimum night temperature of 60°F (15°C). Transplant into the growing positions in border soil, straw bales or growing bags when the true rough leaves appear. Plant at least 2 ft (60 cm) apart.

"All-female" varieties may develop a large number of fruits on the main stem, which can be at the expense of further growth. It may therefore be desirable to remove some, especially in unheated conditions, in order to maintain a balanced plant.

Sow outdoor cucumbers in the open garden when the risk of frost is past, or in April under glass for planting out in early June. Fruits are ready for cutting from late July to September.

Support glasshouse and climbing outdoor varieties with trellis, wires or canes.

Variety choice

Glasshouse (all hybrids)

Brunex (12) Produces fairly high yields of good-quality fruits.
Corona (13) In a heated glasshouse, it gives high yields of very good-quality fruits, but is less well adapted to unheated conditions.
Mildana (10) Total yield only moderate but plants have tolerance to mildew. This disease can be very damaging, especially in an unheated glasshouse.
Pepinex 69 (2, 3, 6, 8, 11, 13, 14, 16, 17) Vigorous plants producing large fruits. Yields moderate. AM 1985.
Petita (3, 6, 7, 9, 11, 12, 14, 17) Gives a larger number of shorter fruits, about 8 in. (20 cm), than the others listed.

Outdoor

Burpee Hybrid (6) Trailing, with dark, fruits about 6 in. (15 cm) long.
Burpless Tasty Green (7–12, 14, 15) Hybrid, climbing, with slender smooth-skinned fruits about 9 in. (23 cm) long. HC 1984.
Bush Crop (7, 8) Compact plant suitable for small gardens or patio containers. Produces slender fruit about 6 in. (15 cm) long.
Conda (11) Trailing gherkin variety which can be picked immature for pickling, or left to produce small fruits about 4 in. (10 cm) long. Very smooth-skinned.
Crystal Apple (2, 3, 9, 12, 14) Trailing producing many small round yellow-skinned fruits.

FENNEL

A crop which is grown particularly in Mediterranean areas. Older varieties are susceptible to bolting if sown too early in this country. In recent years breeders in northern Europe have bred varieties which can be sown sufficiently early to allow the production of well developed bulbs.

Cultivation

Seed should be sown in rows 15 in. (38 cm) apart and when the seedlings are well established, singled to 9 in. (23 cm) within the rows. If transplanted, plants should be set at similar spacing.

Variety choice

Zefa Tardo (13) This variety has good resistance to bolting when sown after 20 June. It produces white well filled bulbs in the autumn from a June sowing.

Zefa Fino (3, 6, 7, 11) Better bolting resistance than Zefa Tardo and can be sown from the second week of June, giving a longer growing season and hence the possibility for better bulb development. This variety can also be sown under protection for planting out from March to mid April, but it should never be sown from after mid April or before the second week of June, otherwise bolting will occur. HC 1987.

FRENCH BEANS

Plant breeders have developed varieties of French beans with a range of pod types – short; long round; and long flat, which are similar in appearance to runner beans. There are also yellow- and purple-podded varieties in addition to green. The short-podded varieties have pods less than 4 in. (10 cm) long, which can be cooked or frozen whole rather than sliced, thus retaining flavour better. All the plants are of bush habit, not climbing, and the pods are stringless when harvested young.

Cultivation

Seed should be sown in late April or early May, so that seedlings emerge after the risk of frost has passed, using sufficient seed to produce 4 plants per square foot (0.09 m²). Plants require warm weather to grow well and cloches placed over them are useful in the early part of the season. Seed may also be sown as late as the end of June to produce a crop in late August and September.

Variety choice

Green-podded

Aramis (11, 16) Thin stringless pods 6–7 in. (15–17 cm) long. HC 1988.
Delinel (8) Very long, slim, stringless pods. AM 1983, 1988.

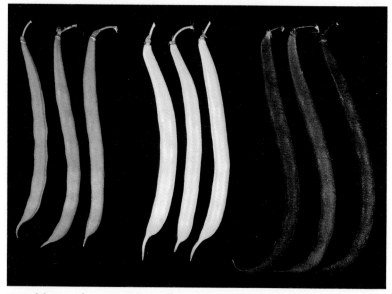

French beans, showing green-, yellow- and purple-podded types

Montano (17) Maturing a few days earlier than Loch Ness. Short to medium length narrow stringless pods with round cross-section.

Pros (Gitana) (6–8, 11) Maturing about 95 days from sowing. Pods 4 in. (10 cm) long, round to oval cross-section, straight, stringless. May be cooked or frozen whole. HC 1983.

Tendergreen (2, 3, 7, 9, 10, 12, 14, 15, 17) Stringless round pods 6–7 in. (15–17 cm) long. HC 1979.

Purple-podded

Purple Queen (7, 9, 11); **Purple Teepee** (7, 10) Purple pods about 6 in. (15 cm) long, stringless.

Yellow-podded

Kinghorn Wax (7, 9) Yellow flattish pods 5–6 in. (12–15 cm) long, containing green seeds. Adds an attractive colour contrast when cooked with green beans.

KALE

Curly kale or borecole is harvested during the late autumn and winter and is renowned as one of the hardiest of vegetables. It produces a mass of very curled and cut leaves which, when cooked, are an attractive dark green and have a good flavour. Plant breeders have concentrated on developing hybrids and these are very uniform plants with densely curled and cut leaves.

Cultivation

Sow the seed in a well prepared seed bed in May, to produce seedlings 1 in. (2.5 cm) apart in rows spaced at 12 in. (30 cm). Plants should be transplanted to their final positions in the garden when they are six to eight weeks old, at a spacing of 18 × 18 in. (45 × 45 cm). Water to establish in dry conditions and to encourage growth in very dry weather.

Variety choice

Darkibor (3, 6) Hybrid. Hardy plants, medium tall with dark green finely curled leaves. For autumn and winter cropping.
Fribor (2, 3, 12, 15) Hybrid. Hardy plants about 8 in. (45 cm) high, maturing from November to February. The leaves are finely curled, deep green and very attractive. AM 1987.

Picking the young leaves and shoots of curly kale

Kohl rabi 'Lanro'

KOHL RABI

A member of the cabbage family, this is an unusual vegetable in that the stem swells up above ground level. Easy to grow but it needs to be harvested tennis ball size, before it gets too large.

Cultivation

Sow April to July outdoors thin to 9 in. (22 cm) apart. Can also be raised in modules and transplanted. Matures in about 12 weeks.

Variety choice

Lanro (6, 7, 16) Green skinned with white flesh. Does not lose quality if harvested after maturity.
Purple Vienna (2, 3, 5, 6, 7, 9, 12, 15, 17) Purple skinned with white flesh.
Rowel (8, 10, 11) Hybrid variety. Green skinned variety with white flesh. Fast maturing. HC 1990.

LEEKS

Leeks may be used throughout the autumn and winter until late spring and they can be left in the ground and lifted as required. The vegetable has received a good deal of attention from plant breeders, with the object of increasing the length of the white stem or shank and improving winter-hardiness.

Cultivation

Sow the seed in March in rows 12–18 in. (30–45 cm) apart in the garden. The seedlings should be thinned to 3–6 in. (7.5–15 cm) apart, according to the size of the leek required, when they have two or three leaves. The alternative method is to sow the seed in a seed bed, also in March, and transplant into the garden in May, in rows 12–18 in. (30–45 cm) apart, with plants spaced at 3–6 in. (7.5–15 cm). To increase the length of blanched stem, the plants should be progressively earthed up during the growing season.

Variety choice (in order of maturity; see also p. 61).

King Richard (3, 6, 8, 11, 17) Maturing in early to mid-autumn, a variety with a shank 10–12 in. (25–30 cm) long and consequently high-yielding. The foliage or flag colour is pale green.
Prelina (13, 16) Maturing in early autumn and suitable for harvesting during the autumn. Shank 8–9 in. (30–22 cm) long. Mid-green flag with little bulbing (swelling at base).
Gennevilliers – Splendid (11) Maturing in early autumn and suitable for harvesting during the autumn. The shank is about 8 in. (20 cm) long and shows some bulbing. HC 1984.
Pancho (6) Maturing in autumn. Shank 8 in. (20 cm) long and slightly bulby, with a mid-green flag.
Swiss Giant – Albinstar (2, 9, 12, 14, 15) For harvesting from autumn to early winter. Long shank with slight bulbing and a medium to light green flag.
Autumn Mammoth 2 – Argenta (6, 10, 12); **Autumn Mammoth 2 – Goliath** (2, 3, 14, 15) Maturing in late autumn and suitable for harvesting through

Leeks 'Winterreuzen', a good late variety for January to March

the winter. In most years they will stand into the spring. The shank is about 5 in. (12 cm) long and shows little bulbing. Attractive leeks producing high yields.

Cortina (10, 13, 16, 17) For harvesting during the winter. Medium length shanks with little bulbing. Medium dark green flag.

Wintra (formerly Winterreuzen) (3) For harvesting from winter to early spring. Shank about 6 in. (15 cm) long, with little bulbing and a medium green flag. AM 1983.

Blauwgroene Winter – Alaska (3, 12) Matures during the spring. Short, very bulby shank with a very dark green flag.

LETTUCE

There are four main types of lettuce – butterhead or round-leaved with soft leaves; crisphead, with crisp wrinkled leaves; Cos, upright-growing, with long thick leaves; and loose-leaved or non-hearting, often with curled leaves.

Plant breeding of butterhead lettuce has produced varieties which heart up well, giving heads of good shape, with resistance to downy mildew. This disease can make the outer leaves unattractive and inedible.

Crisphead lettuce has received less attention from breeders, although new varieties are now becoming available. This type of lettuce is sold in shops as either "Iceberg" or "Webbs" lettuce – a

Lettuce 'Little Gem', *left*, and 'Winter Density', *right*

34

general term describing the way the lettuces are presented (and not meaning that they are actually the varieties 'Iceberg' or 'Webb's Wonderful'). Icebergs are dense, heavily trimmed hearts from which all outer leaves have been removed; Webbs are less densely hearted, with most of the outer leaves retained. Most crisphead varieties are suitable for Webbs use, while some are suitable for Iceberg use if left to grow denser.

By using cold frames and cloches, the harvesting season can be extended and, with a heated glasshouse, lettuce can be produced all the year round. However, it is important to choose varieties appropriate to the purpose.

Cultivation outside

A succession of lettuces can be obtained from June to October by sowing seed at intervals from late March onwards to early July. Some winter-hardy varieties can be sown in September for the following spring.

Seed of butterhead varieties can be sown directly into rows 12 in. (30 cm) apart in the garden, thinning to give a plant at intervals of 10 in. (25 cm). Alternatively, sow in soil blocks for subsequent transplanting at 10 × 12 in. (25 × 30 cm). The latter method allows the seed to be sown in a cold frame or under cloches in March, for planting out in April to achieve an early crop. It should be remembered, however, that the germination of lettuce under glass may be hindered by seed dormancy, owing to the higher temperature. The soil blocks should therefore be watered and stood in a cool shaded place out of doors for 3 days after sowing, before being placed in a glasshouse or frame to germinate the seed.

The same methods can be used for crisphead varieties, but most need a spacing of 12 × 12–15 in. (30 × 30–38 cm).

The commonest pest to affect lettuce is aphid or greenfly, which disfigure the leaves as well as spreading virus diseases. Root aphids can be a problem in hot dry weather. These live on the surface of the roots and stunt the plants, causing them to wilt.

Variety choice

Butterhead (in order of maturity)

Avondefiance (2, 3, 6, 8, 9, 12, 14, 15) For cropping from June to August and will withstand dry conditions and high temperatures well. It produces high yields of good-quality heads, having mid- to dark-green leaves, but with a rather untidy heart and pointed base. Resistant to root aphid and some resistance to downy mildew.

Clarion (3, 13) For cropping from June to October. Leaves mid- to dark-greyish green and thicker than average. Good resistance to tipburn and downy mildew and claimed tolerance to lettuce mosaic virus.

Musette (9, 12) For cropping in June and September to October. Medium to dark green, slightly thicker than average leaves. Good resistance to downy mildew and resistant to lettuce mosaic virus and root aphids.

Pandorian (16) For cropping from June to October. Fairly large, well formed, medium green heads. Good resistance to downy mildew.

Crisphead (in order of maturity)

Minetto (6) For cropping from June until October. Small heads with leaves deeply cut at their margins. Suitable for Webbs and small Iceberg heads only.

Malika (11, 16) For cropping in June and September to October. Fast growing, producing medium-sized dense heads. Can quickly become over-mature. Suitable for Webbs and medium-sized Iceberg heads.

Saladin (2, 3, 6–8, 11–17) For cropping in July to September. Large, dark green heads which are fairly dense and hold better than most varieties. Suitable for Webbs and large Iceberg heads.

Warpath (3, 7, 9) For cropping from June until October. Producing small heads with tight hearts of good texture and flavour. Can be grown at closer spacings than most other Crisphead varieties.

Cos (for cropping from June to October)

Little Gem (2, 3, 6–15, 17) Small Cos type producing tight hearts of excellent flavour. Because of its size, spacing within the row can be reduced to 6 in. (15 cm). Suitable for growing in a cold frame or in the open ground. HC 1978, 1982; AM 1977, 1987, 1990.

Lobjoits Green Cos (2, 3, 7–9, 12, 13, 15, 17) High quality, with well turned in heart, but subject to tipburn, so harvest before head is too dense. Can also be sown in September for maturing in spring. HC 1978; AM 1982, 1987.

Valmaine (2, 10, 12) Duller-looking leaf and does not heart in as well as Lobjoits Green Cos, but less susceptible to tipburn.

Miscellaneous (green leafy, red and winter)

Wallop (7) Leaves fairly small, rather upright, greyish green with a pleasant semi-crisp texture. Heart eventually filling out to give a well filled, round bunch. Holds well in the garden. Because of its size, spacing within the row can be reduced to 7 in. (17 cm).

Salad Bowl (2, 6–9, 11, 12, 14, 15, 17) Non-hearting heads of pale yellow green, deeply divided leaves that can be picked individually. One sowing can therefore be harvested over a long period, though it is usually necessary to have at least two to cover the whole season.

Red Salad Bowl (2, 3, 6, 7, 9, 12, 14, 15) Red-tinged variant of Salad Bowl.

Lollo Rossa (2, 3, 5–14, 16) Non-hearting variety with red-tinged leaves waved and serrated at the edges. An interesting addition to salad. (See p. 34.)

Lollo Bionda (6, 7) Differing from Lollo Rossa only in being pale green without any trace of red pigmentation.

Quattro Stagione (Merveille de Quatre Saisons) (12, 13, 16) Butterhead type with the exposed leaves coloured deep red. Prone to tipburn.

Valdor (2, 6, 8–10, 12, 14, 15) Winter-hardy butterhead variety for sowing in September, maturing in spring.

Winter Density (2, 3, 5–7, 9, 11, 12, 14, 17) Winter-hardy semi-Cos variety. Sow in September for spring crops, spring for summer crops. HC 1978, 1987. (See p. 34.)

Cultivation under glass

Lettuce can now be harvested under glass throughout the year, but the most popular period is November to May. To produce heads between mid-December and February, some heat is generally necessary – night minimum 36°F (2°C), day minimum 40°F (4.5°C).

Sow butterhead varieties from September to mid-October, for cutting from November to February; sow in mid-October, transplanting in mid-November, for February to early April; sow in November and December, transplanting in January and February, for mid-April to early May.

Some crisphead varieties for growing under glass have been developed recently. They cannot cope with such low light conditions as butterheads and over most of the country are only suitable for cropping in November, from an August sowing, and May when sown in February. Heads will not be as dense as outdoor crispheads. Space at 9 × 9 in. (23 × 23 cm).

Variety choice (in order of maturity)

Butterhead

Novita (3, 6, 8, 11) For cutting from November to early April. Non-hearting, producing a rosette of rather frilled, wavy leaves. Slightly crisp.

Columbus (6, 14); **Pascal** (3, 15) For cutting from November to early May. Heads medium-sized and leaves fairly thick. Heads do not become too drawn in midwinter.

Cynthia (7, 11) For cutting from February to early April. Heads fairly large, forming a distinct heart. Grows fast but somewhat softer than others maturing in this period.

Magnet (14, 17) For cutting from mid-April to early May. Heads very large and benefits from a spacing of 9 × 9 in. (23 × 23 cm). Puts on weight very fast but less firm than other varieties.

Crisphead

Marmer (10, 11) For cutting in November. Well shaped hearts with few outer leaves. True crisp texture. AM 1980, HC 1984.

Marbello (7) For cutting in March and April. Paler than most crispheads and fairly slow to develop, but produces good hearts and holds fairly well at this time of year.

Kellys (3, 8, 11, 12, 15) Bright green colour, dense heads with relatively few outer leaves. Same season as Marbello.

MARROW, COURGETTES, SQUASH AND PUMPKIN

Of the large number of edible gourds, courgettes and marrows are the best known. Some varieties have been bred especially to produce many small fruits or courgettes, which are simply immature marrows picked when 4–7 in. (10–17 cm) long. If these are left to grow, they will produce mainly fairly slender marrows. Other varieties have been bred specifically for marrow production, giving rather broader and fewer fruits per plant. The main harvesting season is July to September and both courgettes and marrows should be cut regularly to prolong fruiting. A few marrows can be left on the plants to ripen further and are then removed before frost for winter storage.

Like courgettes, summer squash is picked when the fruits are small and immature. They come in different colours and shapes, including globe, club and round cushion shapes with scalloped edges and crook necks. Cook the same way as courgettes.

Courgettes 'Gold Rush', *left*, and summer squash 'Custard White', *right*

Winter squash is harvested when fully ripe. The shapes and colours are many and various – globe, turban, onion, corn, capstan and marrow shapes and white, orange, green, pale brown and yellow colours. The flesh is usually fine-grained and is eaten baked or in pies. They can be stored for winter use.

The name pumpkin is used in the UK for fruits grown to maturity on the plants. They have a globe or flattened globe shape, often large, and coarse-grained flesh. Pumpkin is used as a pie filler or for ornament or exhibiting and can be stored for the winter.

Cultivation
Sow under glass in May, in seed compost in small pots or soil blocks to achieve one seedling per container. Transplant into the garden as soon as the risk of frost has passed, at a spacing of 3 × 3ft (90 × 90 cm) for bush varieties and 3 × 6 ft (90 × 180 cm) for trailing varieties.

Variety choice

Courgettes

Ambassador (3, 6, 7, 8, 12, 13–15, 17) Hybrid bush type producing many cylindrical green courgettes. Can also be grown on for marrows. HC 1986.
Brimmer (10, 14) Non-hybrid bush type with cylindrical, attractive, green courgettes.
Early Gem (2, 3, 11, 17) Hybrid bush type having cylindrical, dark green fruits with pale flecking. A good variety for courgettes and can also be grown on for marrows. HC 1979, AM 1986.
Gold Rush (2, 5–8, 10, 11, 17) Hybrid bush type, with cylindrical, golden yellow fruits. Very suitable for courgettes, although slightly late to pick. HC 1986.

Marrow

All Green Bush (2, 3, 5, 7, 11, 12, 17) Bush type with green cylindrical fruits.
Long Green Trailing (2, 3, 6–9, 11, 12, 14, 15, 17) Trailing variety producing large marrows with pale and dark green stripes.
Twickers (10) Hybrid semi-trailing type. Producing "rugby ball" shaped green and white striped fruits.
Zebra Cross (8, 13) Hybrid bush type more suitable for marrows than courgettes. The fruits are attractively striped white and green. HC 1988.

Summer squash

Custard White (2, 6, 12, 14, 15) Bush habit. Round cushion-shaped fruits with scalloped edges, about 7 in. (17 cm) in diameter.
Tender and True (2, 9) Bush habit. Round, mottled green fruits. Early to mature.

Winter squash

Butternut (6, 7, 14) Cylindrical fruits 10 in. (25 cm) long with swollen end and small seed cavity. Orange skin and bright orange flesh. Trailing habit.
Hubbard's Golden (9, 17) Oval fruits about 10 in. (25 cm) long. Golden skin and trailing habit. HC 1984.
Table Ace (7, 9) Acorn-shaped, dark green to black fruits, 5 in. (12 cm) long. Yellow flesh. Semi-bush habit. HC 1984.
Vegetable Spaghetti (2, 6, 7, 9, 11, 12, 14, 15, 17) Trailing habit. Narrow-shaped white-skinned fruits, 8–10 in. (20–25 cm) long. The flesh separates into spaghetti-like strands when cooked.

Pumpkin

Mammoth (2, 3, 5–7, 11, 12, 14, 17) Trailing habit. Long, round, orange-skinned fruits.

MELON

Cultivation
Sow in heat in early May in small pots or soil blocks and transplant into growing bags (two or three per bag) or into a well cultivated, fertile border in a glasshouse in late May, when the risk of low night temperatures has passed. Melons can also be grown in cold frames. In the glasshouse, plants may be trained up support mesh and will need stopping. Careful and regular watering and feeding are required for good growth, especially where plants are grown in growing bags.

The female flowers should be pollinated to produce fruit set, but the number of developing fruits should be restricted to encourage the development of good-quality fruits. Melons can usually be harvested from late August to September, when they are easily broken off at the point of attachment between stem and fruit.

Variety choice (all early-maturing)

Charentais (3, 7, 9, 14) Pale, grey green skin and slight netting. Fruits are round with pale orange flesh.

Ogen (2, 3, 6–10, 14, 15, 17) Gives a good yield of small, broad oval fruits, basically green-skinned but with yellow stripes.

Pancha (13) Cream in colour and fully netted when ripe. Fruits round with pale orange flesh. HC 1985.

Sweetheart (2, 3, 6–12, 14, 15, 17) Hybrid, producing a high yield of white smooth-skinned fruits with pinkish orange flesh.

ONIONS

Plant breeding of bulb onions has produced new selections and hybrids of spring-sown varieties, which store well, and hybrids with improved uniformity. Perhaps the most important development has been the introduction of varieties which can be sown in August and over-wintered to produce bulbs in June and July of the following year.

By growing spring-sown onions and storing them, and August-sown onions for maturing during the summer, it is possible to be self-sufficient in this vegetable throughout the year. However, remember that August-sown onions do not store well.

In addition to the more usual brown- or yellow-skinned onions, there are red varieties which can be grown in the same way. Most of the colour is in the skin and outer layers, but they make an interesting colour contrast, particularly when used raw in salads.

Cultivation of spring-sown onions

For maincrop production in early to mid-September, seed should be sown as soon as soil conditions allow in February or March. Use sufficient seed in drills to achieve about five plants per foot (30 cm) of row, in rows 12–15 in. (30–38 cm) apart. For an earlier crop, plants can be started under glass at a temperature of 50–60°F (10–15 °C) in early February. Sow one to five seeds in soil blocks or modules. Lower the temperature gradually to give frost protection and harden off in March. The aim is to produce plants with two true leaves for transplanting in early April.

The most important disease affecting stored onions is neck rot. This can be controlled by sowing seed which has been treated with a seed dressing containing a mixture of benomyl and thiram.

Variety choice (in order of maturity)

Brown-skinned (all store well)

Caribo (10, 13, 16) Hybrid. Thick-skinned, dark straw-coloured bulbs.

Rijnsburger – Balstora (3, 6, 8, 13) Onions with dark thick skins.

Hygro (2, 3, 6, 8, 11, 12, 15, 17) Hybrid variety, vigorous, with globe-shaped bulbs.

Rijnsburger – Robusta (2, 12, 14) Dark straw-coloured bulbs.

Red

Red Baron (2, 6, 10) Globe-shaped selection.

White

Albion (7, 8, 10, 17) Hybrid. Globe shaped. Shorter storage than brown-skinned varieties.

Cultivation of August-sown onions

Seed should be sown during August – the second week of the month in the north; the third week in the Midlands and east; and the fourth week in the south. (These precise dates are critical, in order to avoid the onions either growing too large and bolting in the spring, or being too small and failing to survive the winter.) Sow enough seed to achieve ten plants per foot (30 cm) of row, in rows 12–15 in. (30–38 cm) apart. Some of the seedlings usually die in winter, but if losses have been only slight, then thin the plants to leave 6–8 per foot (30 cm) of row.

Apply sufficient fertilizer in the autumn to encourage slow growth, for if plants become too well grown, they are unlikely to survive the winter. Additional nitrogen fertilizer should be given as soon as the weather improves in the new year, in order to promote early and adequate growth for a satisfactory yield. The harvesting season is from mid-June to mid-July.

Salad onions 'White Lisbon', suitable for all-year-round crops

Variety choice (in order of maturity)

Express Yellow O–X (2, 10, 12, 14) Hybrid variety. Bulbs are semi-flat with moderate yield and thin skins. AM 1978, 1988.
Buffalo (2, 6, 7, 13–15) Hybrid producing a very high yield of globe-shaped bulbs with thin skins.
Keepwell (10) Hybrid. Dark straw-coloured, globe-shaped bulbs with thick skins.
Imai Early Yellow (8) Produces a good yield of globe-shaped onions with yellow skins of moderate thickness.
Senshyu Semi-Globe Yellow (3, 8, 9, 11, 12, 14, 15, 17) High yields of globe-shaped bulbs with fairly thick skins.

ONIONS FROM SETS

Cultivation of Onion Sets

Sets should be planted from February to April leaving only the tops visible 4–6 in. (10–15 cm) within rows, 12–15 in. (30–38 cm) apart.

Variety choice

Sturon (11, 14, 15) Good yield and quality. Slightly flattened bulbs with good skins. Should store until March, and in some seasons longer.

ONIONS, SALAD

Salad or spring onions are grown for their slender white shank and green leaves and used mainly in salads. The traditional varieties still have the best winter-hardiness and freedom from bolting.

Cultivation

Seed is sown from February onwards to give successional cropping during the summer and autumn. Seed may also be sown from mid-August to early September to produce a crop for over-wintering and maturing in April and May. Sufficient seed should be sown to give 20 plants per foot (30 cm) of row, in rows spaced 12–18 in. (30–45 cm) apart.

Variety choice

Hikari (2, 6, 14) A Japanese bunching onion which is not winter hardy. Very pale green leaves. Very little bulbing. Very prone to bolting, but the flower stalks are hollow and so do not detract from the appearance of the bunched produce.

White Lisbon – Winter Hardy (3, 6, 7, 9, 11, 14, 17) The hardiest variety. Good length of white stem and medium to dark green leaf.
White Lisbon (2, 3, 5–17) Paler leaf and less well blanched than White Lisbon – Winter Hardy, but develops bulbs more slowly. AM 1986.

PARSLEY

There are three main types of parsley – the familiar curly-leaved; the plain-leaved or continental; and the Hamburg or turnip-rooted. The first two are used as a culinary herb, while the third is grown both for the leaves and for the long swollen root, which is a useful winter vegetable resembling parsnip and can be used in the same way.

Cultivation

Parsley is a biennial crop best germinated with some heat in March and then kept cool for transplanting in late May. It can also be sown direct in March or April and again in June or July for the autumn. Plants can either be spaced out singly about 6 in. (15 cm) apart in rows, or grown close together for repeated cutting. Many varieties are not winter-hardy and will be killed by hard frosts; those which survive will produce seed stalks in the second year. Plants of Hamburg parsley should be spaced at 10 × 8 in. (25 × 20 cm) to allow full development of the roots. They are ready for harvesting in November and can be left in the ground for lifting as required.

Variety choice

Bravour (3, 11, 14, 15) Curled type with good winter-hardiness. HC 1985.
Curlina (6–8, 11) Moss-curled type.
Hamburg Turnip-Rooted (2, 7, 8, 9, 11, 12, 14, 17) Smooth non-curled leaves and swollen root about 8 in. (20 cm) long.
Plain-Leaved (7–12, 14, 17) Tall, fairly erect variety with smooth non-curled leaves. Plants go to seed at the end of the season.

PARSNIP

Plant breeders have concentrated on breeding for resistance to canker in parsnips. This disease causes black or orange brown rots on the shoulder and crown of the roots and is most serious on peaty soils, but can occur on other soils.

Cultivation

Seed is sown in April or May in shallow rows 18–24 in. (45–60 cm) apart and the plants subsequently thinned to give 3–4 per foot

(30 cm) of row. The roots are usually ready from October onwards and can be left in the soil all winter for use when needed.

Variety choice

Avonresister (3, 7, 8, 10–12, 14, 15, 17) Small bulbous roots. It has cream flesh and is sweeter than other varieties. Good canker-resistance.

Cobham Improved Marrow (6, 8) Medium-sized, mainly wedged-shaped, but with some bayonet-shaped roots. It has smooth skin and white flesh with good resistance to canker. HC 1978.

Gladiator (3, 7, 9, 10) Hybrid variety. Medium to large, uniform, wedge-shaped roots. Smooth skin, white flesh, good canker resistance.

White Gem (2, 3, 8, 9, 11–15, 17) Large wedge-shaped to bulbous roots with smooth skin and white flesh. Good resistance to canker. HC 1978.

White Spear (16) Large uniform, bulbous roots with smooth skin, and good canker resistance.

PEAS

Plant breeding has been directed at producing shorter-growing varieties on which all the pods tend to mature together. This does mean that if only one variety is used, it should be sown in succession to obtain a crop lasting several weeks. Alternatively, a number of varieties maturing at different times can be sown at the same time to spread the harvest from mid-May to early September.

Mangetout peas are varieties where the whole pod can be eaten. There are two basic types – sugar peas, which are eaten as flat immature pods; and snap peas, which have plump fleshy pods.

Resistance to Race 1 of pea wilt has been bred into many of the modern varieties.

Cultivation

Seed can be sown from late February to the middle of May to give a population of 10 plants per square foot (0.09 m^2).

Variety choice

Garden peas (maturing about 102 days from sowing, unless otherwise stated)

Dark-Skinned Perfection (6) Very vigorous variety producing plants over 30 in. (75 cm) tall, bearing dark green peas which freeze well. Resistant to Race 1 of pea wilt (susceptible to Race 2).

Hurst Beagle (2, 7, 8, 11, 15) Maturing about 90 days from sowing. Peas small medium, mid-dark green, of good quality and flavour, freeze well. Plants 20 in. (50 cm) tall. Susceptible to Race 1 of pea wilt. HC 1988.

Hurst Green Shaft (2, 3, 5–12, 14, 15, 17) High yields of dark green peas. Plants 30 in. (75 cm) tall. Resistant to Race 1 of pea wilt.

Poppet (6, 11) Semi-leafless variety about 36 in. (90 cm) tall. It produces dark green, medium-sized peas suitable for freezing. Resistant to Race 1 of pea wilt.

Tristar (6) Medium-sized, medium to dark green peas. Plants about 25 in. (63 cm) tall, bearing pods in clusters of up to three.

Sugar and mangetouts

Oregon Sugar Pod (7–11) A sugar pea about 40–48 in. (100–120 cm) tall. Produces flat pods about 4 in. (10 cm) long Should be eaten young and cooked whole.

Sugar Rae (3, 6, 12, 15) Short-stemmed snap sugar pea, about 30 in. (75 cm) tall. Pods about 4½ in. (11 cm) long. Susceptible to Race 1 of pea wilt.

Sugar Snap (2, 5, 7–10, 12, 14) Long-stemmed snap sugar pea, 48–72 in. (120–180 cm) tall. The pods are only about 3 in. (7.5 cm) long but the plants produce a good yield. Resistant to Race 1 of pea wilt. HC 1986.

POTATOES

The following guidelines should help to ensure success in growing good-quality potatoes:

1. *Buy healthy seed potatoes.* This reduces the risk of virus disease, which rapidly builds up in potatoes grown outside seed-producing areas. Do not save seed from your garden. Certified seed guarantees health as well as trueness to variety.

2. *Sprout seed potatoes before planting.* Sprout in light frost-free conditions. This improves crop emergence and earliness.

3. *Grow on land with good fertility.* High levels of potash are especially beneficial.

4. *Practise good rotation.* This reduces the risk of soil pests.

5. *Lift potatoes as early as possible.* This helps reduce disease, such as potato blight, and pest damage, from slugs.

6. *Store potatoes for eating in a cool, dry, dark place.* Avoid vermin and frost.

7. *Choose the right variety.* Consider maturity, cultivation and eating requirements.

Cooking quality depends on factors related to the variety, weather conditions, soil type and the method of cooking. The varieties referred to below normally cook well, but particular strengths or weaknesses are noted. One of the commonest problems with boiled potatoes is disintegration and this can be minimized either by steaming them in a steamer, or by reducing the quantity of water used when boiling.

Potatoes are grouped according to the season of lifting as earlies ("new" potatoes) and maincrop.

Cultivation

Do not plant until there is little risk of frost. Seed may be planted into ridged or unridged soil, but the growing plants should be earthed up to provide adequate cover for the developing tubers and to prevent the tubers from turning green.

Widths between rows and plant spacing within the row are not critical and may vary with the variety and maturity type, the amount of tilth and expected rainfall. As a general rule, rows should be 24–30 in. (60–75 cm) apart and spacing between plants 12–15 in. (30–38 cm). Plant early varieties more closely than late varieties, as they require less room in the shorter growing period. Planting depth should be about 3–6 in. (7.5–15 cm).

Inspect potatoes regularly and spray against potato blight, especially during warm wet weather in late June, July and August. If blight takes a strong hold, cut down the haulms (stems and leaves) and do not lift the tubers for at least two weeks. Always lift tubers in warm dry conditions and store only sound undamaged tubers in dry, cool, but frost-free conditions.

With early varieties, it is important to use well sprouted seed and plant as early as possible, usually from mid-March. Protect from late frosts, by drawing a little soil over the shoots. Most early varieties are susceptible to potato blight and should therefore be lifted during June and July. Maincrop varieties may be planted later than earlies, in April, and should be lifted as early as possible, in September to October, and stored carefully.

Earlies may be grown under clear polythene, as either a cover or a mulch, to promote early bulking or swelling of the tubers. In most years, a two-week benefit in earliness can be expected. After planting, cover the rows with polythene and anchor it firmly by burying the edges, to prevent wind damage. If using the polythene as a cover, allow potatoes to grow under it for about four weeks after the shoots have emerged and then slit the polythene to enable them to grow normally. If using it as a mulch, slit the material as the shoots emerge and let the tops grow through. Problems may arise from wind damage to the polythene, weeds, frost, particularly after removing the polythene when the plants are "soft", and lack of moisture. Water as soon as the cover is removed, or use a trickle hose down the row under the cover.

One of the main difficulties in small gardens and allotments where lack of space prevents proper three- or four-year rotation of crops, is the build up of potato cyst nematodes. Under certain conditions, these can reduce plant growth, or in heavy infestations result in total failure. However, varieties resistant to the common RO_1 strain are now available.

(For full details of variety identification, see *Potato Varieties*, obtainable from the NIAB).

Variety choice (year of introduction indicated)

Early

Arran Pilot (1930) A late first early that will produce high yields if left later. Sprouts early and rapidly. Good drought resistance. Waxy texture, and a good flavour. Long oval shape. Skin and flesh white.

Epicure (1897) Old early variety that produces moderate yields of deep-eyed tubers with a floury cooked texture. Good frost recovery. Popular in the north of England and Scotland. Shape round. Skin and flesh white.

Foremost (1955) Moderate-yielding first early variety. Poor foliage cover. Cooked texture is rather floury. Shape oval. Skin and flesh white. HC 1986.

Maris Bard (1974) Very early and high yielding. Sprout development is fairly late for a first early and preliminary sprouting of seed will result in an earlier crop. Shape short oval. Skin white and flesh cream.

Pentland Javelin (1968) Slow sprouting and bulks later than some early varieties. Good tuber appearance suitable for exhibiting. Resistant to potato cyst nematode (RO_1 strain). Shape round. Skin white and flesh very white. HC 1980.

Rocket (1989) Very early bulking, producing an attractive sample of uniform tubers. Resistant to RO_1 strain of potato cyst nematode and partially resistant to the PA 2/3 strain. Very susceptible to tuber blight. Shape round, skin white, flesh white.

Second early

Estima (1973) High yielding, early-bulking, second early variety. Good cooking and keeping qualities. Heavy crop at later lifts. Attractive smooth-skinned tubers. Good drought and blight-resistance. Shape oval. Skin yellow and flesh light yellow.

Marfona (1972) High yielding, second early variety. Tends to produce large tubers but bulks up fairly early. Good drought resistance. Cooking quality is good for boiling and baking. Susceptible to slug damage. Shape short oval to oval. Skins light yellow and flesh cream to light yellow. AM 1981.

Nadine (1987) New second early variety, producing high yields of uniform, attractive, smooth-skinned tubers. Suitable for exhibiting. Susceptibility to drought may produce medium sized tubers. Resistant to potato cyst nematode (RO_1 strain). Firm texture. Shape round to oval. Skin white and flesh cream.

Wilja (1972) High-yielding second early variety. Produces a large number of tubers per plant. Fairly susceptible to drought. Tubers tend to grow near the surface, so good ridging up essential to prevent greening. Waxy texture with good cooking qualities. Shape oval to long oval, occasionally hooked. Skin and flesh light yellow.

Maincrop

Cara (1976) High-yielding late maincrop that produces an attractive uniform sample of pink-eyed tubers. The haulm is very late to mature and sprouted seed will ensure an earlier crop. Susceptible to slug damage. Resistant to potato blight and cyst nematode (RO$_1$). Ideal for jacket baking. Shape round. Skin white with pink eyes and flesh cream.

Desiree (1962) High-yielding, red-skinned, early maincrop. Tuber shape may be irregular on heavy soils. Susceptible to common scab. A very consistent performer with good all round cooking quality. Shape oval. Skin red and flesh light yellow.

Maris Piper (1963) High-yielding, white-skinned maincrop with attractive tubers. Fairly drought-susceptible and susceptible to common scab and slug damage. Resistant to potato cyst nematode (RO$_1$). Very good cooking quality, suitable for French fries. Shape short oval. Skin white, and flesh cream.

Pentland Squire (1970) Very high yielding early maincrop. Large tubers of good quality. Susceptible to hollow heart. High seed rate will prevent tubers getting too big. Some resistance to slugs. Shape short oval. Skin and flesh white.

Romano (1978) High-yielding early maincrop giving uniform red tubers. Susceptible to drought. Good blight resistance. Shape round to short oval. Skin red and flesh cream. AM 1981.

Special use

Pink Fir Apple (1900) A very old maincrop variety, producing low yields of long thin often knobbly shaped tubers. Poor foliage cover. Waxy texture, ideal for salad use or diced cold. Shape very long oval. Skin pink with deep eyes and flesh yellow.

RADISHES

There are two main types of radish. The small quick-grown salad types, usually with all red or red and white skins, are well known. Less familiar are the much larger slower-growing types, often with long cylindrical roots. These include long white summer radishes, sold in shops as mooli or daikon, and winter radishes. The latter can be left in the ground during the winter, protected with straw, and harvested when required, or lifted and stored in sand; they are cooked as a root vegetable.

Cultivation

Salad radishes can be sown in succession from March to September, either in narrow rows or broadcast. They will mature in four to six weeks from these sowing dates. The large long white and winter radishes require a longer growing period and more space. Sow at the end of May or early June for late summer use, or July for winter use. Space seed at 12 in. (30 cm) apart.

Variety choice

Salad

Crystal Ball (9) Traditional round red type, slow to become pithy. HC 1983.
French Breakfast (2, 3, 5–12, 14, 15, 17) Short cylinder shape, 1½–2 in. (4–5 cm) long, red with a white tip. HC 1983.
Long White Icicle (2, 3, 6–9, 11, 14, 15, 17) Smaller version of the long white type which will grow much more quickly in the summer months.
Pink Beauty (6, 9, 17) Round radish with a pink skin.
Sparkler (2, 6, 7, 9, 12, 14, 17) Round red as Crystal Ball, but with a white tip at the root end.

Long white and winter (all long white icicle-shape, 12 in. (30 cm) long)

April Cross (7, 8, 10, 11) Deeply cut, grey green leaves. Late to bolt and slow to go pithy.
Mino Early (6, 9, 17) Deeply cut, medium green leaves. Bolts slightly earlier than others listed. Can be used as winter radish.
Minowase Summer No. 2 (2, 3, 12, 14, 15) Narrow, deeply cut leaves. Roots stay firm without going pithy, late to bolt.

RUNNER BEANS

Plant breeders efforts have been aimed at producing varieties which are stringless. Other varieties become stringy when fully mature, but can be eaten young to avoid this. Regular picking will result in a continuous crop, from about the end of July. Runner beans freeze well.

Cultivation

Runner beans should be given a warm sheltered position, to minimize damage to the pods by wind, and one where bees are likely to be active, to ensure good pollination of the flowers.

Sow after the risk of frost damage to the emerging seedlings has passed. Seed should be sown 6 in. (15 cm) apart in double rows 2 ft (60 cm) apart. Most varieties are climbing and require support, preferably erected before sowing. 8 ft (2.4 m) canes should be set

Dwarf runner beans 'Pickwick', with red flowers, and climbing and white-flowered varieties at the NIAB trials

12 in. (30 cm) apart in each row and tied together between the rows at about 12 in. (30 cm) from the top; two plants are then trained up each cane. Alternatively, a wigwam of canes can be made.

Variety choice

Non-stringless

Bokki (6, 7) Red flowers and pods 11–12 in. (28–30 cm) long.
Enorma (3, 6–10, 13–15) Red flowers and pods 14–15 in. (35–38 cm) long. HC 1976, AM 1983.
Liberty (14) Red-flowered, with very long pods 18–20 in. (45–50 cm) long.

Stringless

Butler (9, 10, 12, 14) Red flowers and pods 9–10 in. (23–25 cm) long.
Desiree (2, 7, 8, 10, 12, 14) White-flowered, with white seeds and pods 11–12 in. (28–30 cm) long. HC 1976, 1983.
Pickwick (7–9, 11, 15, 17) Dwarf variety with red flowers and pods 8–9 in. (20–23 cm) long.
Polestar (7–9, 11, 17) Red flowers and pods about 12 in. (30 cm) long. HC 1983.
Red Knight (2, 3, 7, 8, 12, 16) Red-flowered, with pods 10–11 in. (25–28 cm) long, straight to slightly curved. AM 1983.

SHALLOTS

Single bulbs are planted and these divide at the base to produce a cluster of bulblets inside a single skin.

Cultivation

Plant from January to the end of April, 6 in. (15 cm) apart, in rows 12 in. (30 cm) wide. Harvest in July.

Variety choice

Dutch Yellow (10, 11, 14, 15) Elongate, straw coloured shallots with good storage potential.

Sante (6, 15) Globe shaped reddish to brown skinned shallots. High yields later maturing than Dutch Yellow.

Hative de Niort (2, 8, 9) Large, uniform globe shaped shallots with brown skins. Often used for exhibitions.

SPINACH BEET AND CHARD

Spinach beet, also known as perpetual spinach, and chard, or Swiss chard, belong to the beetroot family. However, the leaves, not the roots, are usually eaten, being cooked in the same way as spinach. With chard, the thick fleshy midribs and swollen leaf stalks also can be steamed or boiled as a separate vegetable.

'Rhubarb Chard', *left*, a very decorative vegetable, and sweet corn 'Candle', *right*, a supersweet variety with long cobs

Cultivation

Sow from April to August for a succession of crops from August to November and through the winter. The seed should be sown in shallow drills about 18 in. (45 cm) apart and after emergence the plants thinned to about 10 in. (25 cm) within the rows. Apply liberal quantities of farmyard manure or use an alternative source of nitrogen fertilizer and water in dry weather.

Variety choice

Spinach beet

Perpetual Spinach (3, 5–9, 10–15) Pale green midribs and medium green leaves.

Chard

Fordhook Giant (8, 11) Very thick, fleshy, white midribs and dark green, curly leaves.
Rhubarb Chard (2, 3, 5–7, 9, 10, 12, 14, 15, 17) Bright red midribs and crumpled green leaves. Good flavour. Also ornamental. (See opposite.)

SWEET CORN

Sweet corn is a tender plant which does best in warm and sheltered areas. Soil temperatures of 50°F (10°C) are required for good establishment and rapid growth. The best conditions occur east of a line from the Isle of Wight to the Wash. In areas further north and west, early varieties give the most reliable production.

The most recent innovation has been the development of varieties with sweeter cobs, called supersweets. Most of these are less vigorous than normal varieties and need later sowings when conditions are warmer. Supersweet varieties should not be grown with traditional varieties, otherwise the sweetness of their cobs will be reduced by cross-pollination.

Cultivation

Seed can be sown directly into the garden when the soil is warm enough, usually from early to mid-May depending on the part of the country. Sow to achieve one plant every 10 in. (25 cm) in rows 30 in. (75 cm) apart, arranged in a square block. Sweet corn is wind pollinated and it is advisable to grow plants in as near square beds as possible to ensure that all the flowers are pollinated so that they produce well filled cobs with straight rows of grain.

Seed can also be sown under glass in April, for transplanting outside as soon as the risk of frost has passed. This compensates for the slow start. Always sow a single seed to a pot or container, as growth can be delayed if the taproot is damaged when separating plants. Cloches or polythene covers are very beneficial to the early growth of sweet corn. The cobs normally mature from July to October according to variety.

Variety choice (all hybrids, in order of maturity)

Traditional varieties

Pilot (13); **Sunrise** (6, 8, 10) Maturing about 120 days from sowing. Half the produce at least 6in. (15 cm) of grain.
Earlibelle (9) Maturing about 125 days from sowing, with well-filled cobs. HC 1988.
Sundance (2, 6, 9, 11) Midseason maturity, with a high yield of well filled medium-sized cobs. HC 1988.
Jubilee (16, 17) Late variety with very good quality cobs.

Supersweet varieties

These varieties contain up to twice the level of sugar found in the traditional sweetcorn varieties. They also remain sweeter for longer when mature. High sugar content makes seeds of these varieties more susceptible to fungal attack when sown, and may therefore be less vigorous when sown in cold wet soils.

Candle (9); **Sweet Nugget** (3, 6) Maturing about 125 days from sowing. Supersweet varieties with very long cobs. Do not always fill to the tip but cobs quite heavy. AM 1987 (Candle).
Conquest (10) Early maturity with well filled cobs.
Sweet 77 (2, 3, 12, 14) Later maturity than 'Candle'. Moderate yield of very large cobs. Early vigour often poor. AM 1987.
Dynasty (10, 13) Late maturing well filled cobs with excellent eating quality.

Supersweet bi-color

Two's Sweeter (10) Cobs contain both white and yellow grain. Late maturing with excellent eating quality.

SWEET PEPPER

Trends in sweet peppers have been towards producing earlier-maturing varieties, which are more suitable for the British climate, and fruits with thicker walls and relatively square in cross section (described as blocky).

Cultivation

Sweet peppers and the smaller hot-flavoured chili peppers are best grown under glass. Plants should be raised from a sowing in mid-March at a temperature of about 60°F (15°C) and pricked off into small pots or soil blocks. Lower the temperature progressively to harden the plants off, prior to transplanting into an unheated glasshouse or cold frame, in early May in the south, or mid- to late May in the north of England. They can be grown in large pots or growing bags. Water plants carefully to avoid waterlogging and feed regularly once the fruits start to swell.

Peppers are usually ready for picking from the end of July until early October. Except where otherwise stated, the varieties mentioned below produce green fruits, which ripen to a bright red if allowed to remain on the plant. However, leaving them will reduce the number of fruits set per plant.

Variety choice (in order of maturity)

Sweet pepper

Canape (6, 10, 11) High-yielding, early-maturing variety with thin-walled fruits tending to be round in cross-section and slightly elongated. HC 1983.
New Ace (3, 7, 12, 17) Hybrid variety cropping early and producing thin-walled blocky fruits. AM 1976.
Bendigo (17) Hybrid variety. Early maturing, giving high yields of thick-walled moderately blocky fruit.
Bellboy (2, 3, 6, 12–16) Hybrid giving high yields of large, thick-walled, blocky fruits. Slightly later than Canape and New Ace. AM 1976, HC 1983.
Luteus (3, 9) Green fruits ripening to clear yellow. Fruits are large, thick-walled and blocky.

TOMATOES

Plant breeders have concentrated on incorporating resistance to leaf mould, verticillium wilt and tomato mosaic virus into modern varieties, as well as improving shape and colour. Although flavour has been a minor consideration, there is little indication that new varieties are inferior in this respect. Varieties do differ in flavour, but the method of growing (especially watering and nutrition) and the amount of sunlight also have a major effect on flavour.

Cultivation

For growing under heated glass, sow in heat, about 60°F (15°C) in December or January. Prick out into pots or soil blocks and, when the plants are of suitable size, in late February or early March, transplant into their final positions at a spacing of 18 in. (45 cm) between each. They can be harvested in May and June.

For growing in a cold glasshouse and outside, sow seed in a temperature of about 60°F (15°C), from mid-March to early April, and prick out into pots or soil blocks when the seedlings are large enough to handle. Plants should be gradually hardened off before transplanting into a cold glasshouse or a sheltered position in the open garden, as soon as the risk of frost has passed, at a spacing of 18 × 18 in. (45 × 45 cm). Outdoor tomatoes should ripen in mid-August and will be slightly earlier under glass. All types may be grown in growing bags and large pots.

Variety choice (small, normal, large and yellow fruits)

Glasshouse

Gardeners Delight (2, 3, 5–12, 14, 15, 17) Small fruits of excellent flavour. AM 1990.
Sweet 100 (7, 9–12, 14, 16, 17) Hybrid small-fruited variety similar to Gardener's Delight.
Abunda (3, 1 4); **Sonatine** (2, 3, 14) Hybrids for growing in heat under glass. High yields of nicely shaped fruits and good disease-resistance.
Danny (2, 3, 7, 14, 17) Hybrid for unheated cropping. Fruits fairly well shaped and yields very high, but shape less good early in the season when grown in heat.
Shirley (2, 3, 7–15, 17) Hybrid similar to Danny. Yields slightly lower but stems a little shorter, which can be useful where headroom is restricted. AM 1990.
Dombito (2, 3, 8, 10, 13) Hybrid with large beefsteak fruits on fairly compact plants. Pinch off the rest of each truss once four fruits are swelling. HC 1990.
Golden Sunrise (2, 3, 5–7, 9, 10, 12, 14, 15, 17) Yellow, medium small fruits.

Outdoor

Alfresco (2, 3, 6, 15). HC 1989. **Red Alert** (2, 3, 6–8, 10–12, 14, 15, 17). AM 1982, HC 1989. **Sleaford Abundance** (2, 8, 14). Hybrid varieties having a bush habit and therefore requiring no training or staking. Small fruits of good quality and flavour. AM 1981, HC 1982.
Gardeners Delight. HC 1982. **Sweet 100.** HC 1990. See above. (Gardeners Delight).

TURNIP AND SWEDE

Plant breeders have concentrated mainly on producing agricultural varieties with high dry matter (i.e. solids rather than water content) and better disease-resistance. For garden use, lower dry matter varieties are preferred, although high dry matter varieties have better frost-hardiness. Turnips may be flat, round or long in shape, with white or yellow flesh, while swedes are generally yellow-fleshed. Turnip tops can also be eaten as greens.

Cultivation

Sow from March to mid-July to give 3 plants per foot (30 cm) of row, with rows about 1 ft (30 cm) apart. Both crops are susceptible to powdery mildew in dry conditions. Roots are produced from May to October and may be left in the ground until December.

Variety choice

Turnip

Golden Ball (Golden Perfection) (Orange Jelly) (3, 6–9, 11, 14, 15, 17) Small globe-shaped roots which have yellow skin and flesh. The short mid-green foliage is of the cut-leaf type. AM 1979, HC 1982.

Manchester Market (2, 3, 8, 13, 14, 16, 17) Round roots with green skin and white flesh. Leaves are cut-leaf type. HC 1982.

Purple Top Milan (3, 6, 7, 9, 11, 14, 15, 17) Early flat roots with purple skin and white flesh. Leaves are strap-leaf type. HC 1982, 1990.

Snowball (2, 3, 5, 8–12, 14, 15, 17) Round roots with white skin and flesh. Leaves are cut-leaf type.

Tokyo Cross (6, 7, 10, 12–14) Hybrid variety producing small to medium, very uniform, globe-shaped roots which have white skin and flesh. Erect foliage is strap-leaf type. May bolt if sown before June. Can mature quickly in about 35 days. AM 1979, 1990.

Swede (all yellow-fleshed)

Acme (3, 5, 6, 7, 12, 14) Round roots with light purple skin. Small tops susceptible to powdery mildew. Medium low dry matter content.

Devon Champion (15) Round roots with purple skin.

Marian (2, 3, 6–9, 11–15) Round roots with light purple skin. Medium-sized tops. More resistant to powdery mildew than Acme. Resistant to club root on most sites. Medium high dry matter content.

TABLE 2

Table 2: cabbage varieties for summer and autumn

Group/Variety	Sowing date	Transplanting date	Spacing of plants	Maturity time (...... = length of time heads can stand in the garden before deteriorating)
Early summer	mid-February (with heat)	mid-April	18 × 9 in. (45 × 23 cm)	June–July
Hispi				
Spivoy				
Spitfire				
Golden Cross				
Derby Day				
Late summer	mid-March	early May	18 × 9 in. (45 × 23 cm)	July–September
Golden Cross				
Derby Day				
Stonehead				
Castello				
Minicole				
Summer red	mid-March	early May	18 × 9 in (45 × 23 cm)	July–September
Langedijk Red Early – Norma				
Ruby Ball				

TABLE 1

Autumn Rapier Hawke	mid-May	end June	24 × 15 in. (60 × 38 cm)
Winter white Hidena Polinius Marathon	late April	early June	24 × 15 in. (60 × 38 cm)
Autumn red Autoro Hardoro	late April	early June	24 × 15 in. (60 × 38 cm)

September	October	November	December	January	February	March
Oliver						
Peer Gynt						
		Dolmic				
		Roger				
		Widgeon				
			Rampart			
				Troika		
					Fortress	

Table 1: maturity range of brussels sprouts varieties

Table 3: cabbage varieties for winter and spring

TABLE 3

Group/Variety	Sowing date	Transplanting date	Spacing of plants	Maturity time ...... = length of time heads can stand in the garden before deteriorating
Savoy/White Celtic Tundra	late May	early July	24 × 15 in. (60 × 38 cm)	November–January
Savoy Ice Queen Wirosa Alaska Wivoy	late May	early July	24 × 15 in. (60 × 38 cm)	October–March
January King January King – Hardy Late Stock 3 Winterton	late May	early July	24 × 15 in. (60 × 38 cm)	October–February
Spring – greens Durham Early Avoncrest Duncan	early August	late September	15 × 5 in. (38 × 13 cm)	April–May

TABLE 5

Offenham 1 – Myatts Offenham Compacta	early August	late September	15 × 10 in. (38 × 25 cm)
Spring – hearted Avoncrest Duncan			
Offenham 1 – Myatts Offenham Compacta Dorado Spring Hero	late August	early October	18 × 12 in. (45 × 30 cm)

Table 5: maturity range of leek varieties

September	October	November	December	January	February	March	April	May
	King Richard							
	Prelina							
	Gennevilliers – Splendid							
	Franse Zomer – Pancho							
	Swiss Giant – Albinstar							
			Autumn Mammoth 2 – Argenta					
			Autumn Mammoth 2 – Goliath					
					Cortina			
					Wintra			
						Blauwgroene Winter – Alaska		

TABLE 4

Table 4: cauliflower varieties all the year round

Group/Variety (* = Walcheren Winter)	Sowing date	Transplanting date	Spacing of plants	Maturity time
Winter for spring heading Asmer Snowcap March *WW3 – Armado April *WW3 – Thanet *WW4 – Markanta *WW3 – Maystar Asmer Pinnacle Vilna	late May	mid-July	26 × 24 in. (66 × 60 cm)	March–June (marks in April, May, June)
Purple Purple Cape	late May	mid-July	26 × 24 in. (66 × 60 cm)	March
Early summer Montano Alpha 3 Paloma White Summer	early October	mid-March	24 × 18 in. (60 × 45 cm)	June
Summer Plana Dok White Rock	mid-March	mid-May	24 × 18 in. (60 × 45 cm)	July–August

TABLE 4

Early autumn			
Plana	late April	mid-June	24 × 20 in. (60 × 50 cm)
White Rock			
Autumn			
Plana	mid-May	late June	26 × 24 in. (66 × 60 cm)
White Rock			
Wallaby			
Barrier Reef			
Canberra			
Serrano	early June	late July	26 × 24 in. (66 × 60 cm)
Green and purple			
Limelight	mid-May	late June	26 × 24 in. (66 × 60 cm)
Romanesco			
Violet Queen	early June	mid-July	26 × 24 in. (66 × 60 cm)

Suppliers

1 Excluded because catalogue withdrawn.
2 J. W. Boyce, Bush Pasture, Lower Carter St, Fordham, Ely, Cambs
3 D. T. Brown & Co Ltd, Poulton Le Fylde, Blackpool FY6 7HX
4 Excluded because catalogue withdrawn.
5 Chiltern Seeds, Bortree Stile, Ulverston, Cumbria LA12 7PB
6 Samuel Dobie & Son Ltd, Broomhill Way, Torquay, Devon TQ2 7QW
7 Mr Fothergill's Seeds, Kentford, Newmarket, Suffolk CB8 7QB
8 S. E. Marshall & Co Ltd, Regal Rd, Wisbech, Cambs PE13 2RF
9 Suttons Seeds, Hele Rd, Torquay, Devon TQ2 7QJ
10 Thompson & Morgan, London Rd, Ipswich, Suffolk IP2 0BA
11 Unwins Seeds Ltd, Histon, Cambridge CB4 4LE
12 Chase Organics (GB) Ltd, Addlestone, Weybridge, Surrey
13 Proseeds, 26 Chapman Close, Potton, Sandy, Beds SG19 2PL
14 Country Gardens, 69/71 Main St, East Leake, Leics LE12 6PF
15 Edwin Tucker & Sons Ltd, Brewery Meadow, Stonepark, Ashburton TQ13 7DG
16 Breeders Seeds Ltd, 17 Summerwood Lane, Halsall, Ormskirk, Lancs L39 8RQ
17 W. W. Johnson & Son Ltd, London Road, Boston, Lincs PE21 8AD

Runner beans trained on a wigwam of canes make an attractive feature